CATERPILLAROLOGY

CATERPILLAROLOGY

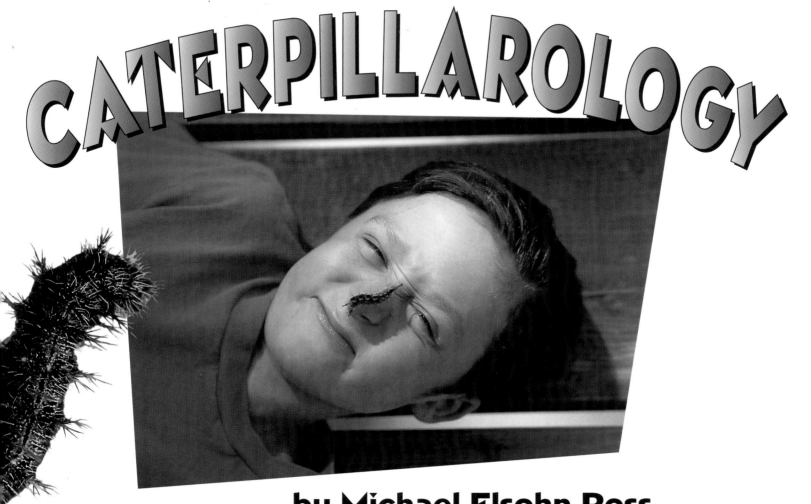

by Michael Elsohn Ross
photographs by Brian Grogan • illustrations by Darren Erickson

Carolrhoda Books, Inc. / Minneapolis

To Ali—may you always be a caterpillar pal

Text copyright © 1997 by Michael Elsohn Ross
Photographs copyright © 1997 by Brian Grogan
Illustrations copyright © 1997 by Carolrhoda Books, Inc.
Photos on pp. 33, 35, 43 courtesy of Robert and Linda Mitchell, © 1997

Carolrhoda Books, Inc., c/o The Lerner Publishing Group
241 First Avenue North, Minneapolis, MN 55401 U.S.A.
Website address: www.lernerbooks.com

LIBRARY OF CONGRESS CATALOGING-IN-PUBLICATIONS DATA

Ross, Michael Elsohn
   Caterpillarology / by Michael Elsohn Ross ; photographs by Brian Grogan ; illustrations by Darren Erickson.
      p.   cm.—(Backyard buddies)
   Includes index.
   Summary: Provides instructions for finding, collecting, and keeping caterpillars and suggests how to delve into the secret lives of these little neighbors of ours.
      ISBN 1-57505-055-2 (alk. paper)
      1. Caterpillars—Juvenile literature. 2. Caterpillars—Experiments—Juvenile literature.
3. Caterpillars as pets—Juvenile literature. [1. Caterpillars as pets. 2. Caterpillars—
Experiments. 3. Experiments.] I. Grogan, Brian, 1951– ill. II. Erickson, Darren, ill. III.
Title. IV. Series: Ross, Michael Elsohn, 1952– Backyard buddies.
QL544.2.R665 1997
595.78'139—dc21   97-1272

Manufactured in the United States of America
1 2 3 4 5 6 – JR – 02 01 00 99 98 97

Contents

Can you munch, munch, munch?

Can you grow, grow, grow?

Do you go slow, slow, slow

like a caterpillar?

Welcome to Caterpillarology

Have you ever met a caterpillar? Caterpillars are the **larvae** (LAR-vee), or early stage, of butterflies and moths. Perhaps you have seen one cruising across the sidewalk or resting on a leaf. When a caterpillar is on the move, it often stops and waves its head back and forth before continuing. Next time you encounter one, why not wave back?

Some folks are scared by these gentle creatures, and others think of them as nasty, plant-eating pests. It's true that caterpillars are hungry leaf munchers. It's also correct that a few kinds of caterpillars protect themselves with chemical weapons. Regardless, there's no need to fear these little critters, since compared to them we are giants.

Paleontology is the study of ancient life, such as dinosaurs, and zoology is the study of animals. Caterpillarology is the study of caterpillars. To be a caterpillarologist, you don't need to hurt or kill anything. All that's necessary is an interest in gently exploring the lives of these little neighbors.

The best time of year to look for caterpillars is in the spring or summer when plants have fresh green leaves. Try looking for caterpillars on leaves, on branches, or cruising along the ground. If you had elephant ears, you might be able to locate your local caterpillars by listening to them munch backyard leaves. They are champion eaters, and this hungry habit leaves lots of clues for caterpillar detectives. As caterpillars chew plants, they make holes. The bits of leaf go in the front end, and out the back come little brown pellets of digested leaves, called **frass**. These droppings are deposited all over cars and anything else that is underneath plants where caterpillars dine. Next time you notice some frass (it looks like brown dandruff), look up and you may discover a well-fed caterpillar.

Backyard Munchers

As caterpillars feed, they sometimes build silk shelters or make silken ropes to lower themselves onto new leaves. Next time you go on a caterpillar hunt, remember to look for bits of silk.

Most caterpillars are harmless, so you need not worry about holding them. A few kinds, including gypsy moth caterpillars, have stinging hairs. If you touch these, you'll get a slight stinging sensation, but this can be avoided by wearing gloves next time you handle them. However, very few hairy caterpillars require this careful handling.

Before you carry some caterpillars home, consider your folks. If they get freaked out by little critters, you might want to show them this article from the *Sun Star Examiner* (a respected make-believe newspaper) before asking permission to host caterpillar guests.

Sun Star Examiner

Great Guests

NEW HOPE, MN—Recently, the Larson family of First Avenue were the proud hosts of some very well-behaved guests. Mrs. Larson reported, "We've hosted cousins, aunts and uncles, and even exchange students from Borneo. They've all been okay, but they don't hold a candle to the cute little caterpillars that my two kids, Elmo and Irma, brought in from the backyard. These caterpillars are quiet, don't leave towels on the floor, and eat very little. Besides, my kids spend so much time watching the little critters that they hardly have time to fight with each other."

Taking care of caterpillars is kind of like being a farmer. Like most farm animals, they need fresh food and the safety of a roof overhead. But to house a caterpillar, you don't need a real barn. A plastic jar with holes in the lid will do just fine.

In their barn, your caterpillars will need plenty of fresh leaves to eat. When you collect your caterpillars, be sure to note the type of leaves that you found them on. Gather a handful of these leaves for them to eat. To keep the leaves fresh, wrap a wet paper towel around the stems and secure it with a rubber band.

Did you ever notice that barns stink? That's because of manure. To keep your barn sweet-scented, clean out the caterpillar manure, also known as frass. Remove the caterpillars every

Caterpillar Barn

few days and rinse out the jar. When you put the caterpillars back in, put them on a new bunch of fresh leaves. Always use the same kind of leaves.

For the safety of your guests, make sure you keep the jar out of direct sunlight. A jar placed in sunlight can get as hot as a greenhouse. Too much heat can harm or even kill your guests. For fun, you can make a sign saying "Caterpillar Barn" to alert your housemates to the new guests. Like other guests, your caterpillars might be happiest in their real home. After a while, you should return them to the plant where you first found them.

Warning: Do not collect caterpillars in parks or preserves where collecting is not allowed.

Although caterpillars might not be as active as a strutting hen or as loud as a rooster, they are still fascinating creatures to watch. Most caterpillars, in fact, move so slowly that as you watch them, you can pretend everything is in slow motion. Try to imagine what it would be like to hang out on a leaf and loll about. The more you watch your caterpillars, the more you can learn to act like them. This could really impress your family

Farmyard Antics

and friends. On the other hand, if you start munching the carpet or spinning a web on the couch, they may think you've gone a bit too far.

• Can you imitate a feeding caterpillar?
• Can you demonstrate how a caterpillar would react to a mild earthquake?
• Can you cruise like a caterpillar?
• What else can you do that a caterpillar does?

As you clean your caterpillar barn, you can provide some entertainment for your guests. Perhaps you could make a caterpillar playpark! A plastic washtub with a layer of soil on the bottom makes a fine park. All that's needed is some play equipment. Consider what caterpillars might enjoy crawling on. Here are a few ideas to get you started (but it's likely that you're already planning some crazy designs of your own).

Caterpillar Playpark

hide? If you think it would enjoy company, add some more caterpillars. Do they notice each other? Do they do the same things? Jot down some notes about their activities and encourage your friends or family to add their observations.

Have you ever thought of yourself as a giant tree? Place a caterpillar on your arm. Can it climb up?

When playtime is over, return your guests to their cozy caterpillar barn. They may need a snack and some rest after all the exercise.

You will need:

✔ marbles
✔ leaves
✔ toy cars
✔ sticks
✔ string
✔ paper tubes

Set a caterpillar in your completed playpark and see what happens. Does it climb, crawl, or

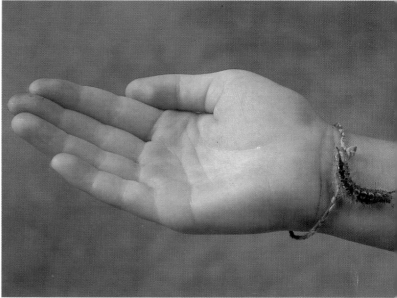

Are you aware? Would you notice if your sister shaved her head or your dog wore a dress? Would you notice if your teacher got braces? Do you pick up on small details? Whatever your answers, the Aware Dare is for you. If you are completely tuned out, this game will help you tune into tiny details. Being tuned in is extremely helpful when you are becoming familiar with new friends, such as caterpillars. On the other hand, if you are totally aware, this game will allow you to show off your remarkable talents. Though it can be played alone, the Aware Dare is more challenging with two or more players.

How to Play

1. Decide on the order of play. *Optional:* pick one player to record what each of you notices.

2. Place a caterpillar in a dish and examine it closely.

3. Beginning with player number 1, take turns sharing observations. For example, a player might say, "It's hairy," or "It wiggles." Any observation is okay, but no repeats are allowed. However, more items can be added to a previous description. For example, though someone may have already said, "It's hairy," another person can add, "Its hairs are red."

4. Continue taking turns in the same order until only one player is able to come up with a new observation. The last person to share a caterpillar characteristic is the most aware.

You will need:

✔ one caterpillar
✔ a magnifying lens
✔ optional: pen or pencil and paper
✔ a plastic bowl or dish

Many things look simple at first glance. To some people, caterpillars may appear like plain little worms, but it's not hard to prove them wrong. As you know, caterpillars aren't worms at all, even though people have given some of them names like army worm and hornworm.

Caterpillars are composed of detailed parts that come in many shapes, colors, and numbers. If you take a close look at them, you can count on caterpillars for some complex anatomy.

The tools listed below will be handy in detecting the details of your small guests.

Counting on Caterpillars

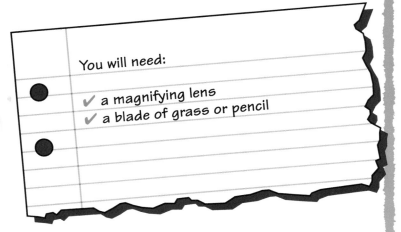

You will need:

✔ a magnifying lens
✔ a blade of grass or pencil

Take a careful look at your caterpillar. How many legs can you find? Can you see a mouth?

What shape is it? Can you see eyes or a nose? What other parts can you examine and count?

How many colors are you wearing today? How many colors is your caterpillar wearing? What shapes or patterns can you see? After your examination is over, share your discoveries with friends or family. You may be able to teach them a thing or two about "simple" little caterpillars.

Modeling for an artist is not an easy task. The model must remain in one pose for hours while the artist sketches, paints, or sculpts. Slow-moving creatures such as caterpillars make perfect models. They do not charge a modeling fee, and they can even eat while posing without causing a great stir. It's a wonder that there are not more caterpillar portraits in art museums. Maybe you can correct this unfair situation by using your caterpillar as a model for your next portrait.

Munching Models

race car driver, a giant serpent attacking a house, or anything else you want.

1. Fly with your Eyes: Using the hand lens, pretend you are a helicopter flying over the caterpillar. Carefully examine its colors, shapes, parts, and other details such as hairs, bumps, and ridges.

2. Snapshot: Make some quick, simple sketches of the different things that you notice, such as the shape of the caterpillar's head or the position of its eyes.

3. Regard Your Curiosity: If questions such as, "What is that thing called?" pop into your brain, jot them down next to your drawings. Questions are well worth collecting.

4. Almost There. . . : Before making the final picture, do some loose sketches of the basic shape of the caterpillar. This will help you to experiment with the picture before setting to work on the fine details.

5. Bigger Than Life: Drawing a life-size caterpillar is a challenge. It's easier to include small details when you make your artwork big. Give your portrait plenty of room.

6. Art Show: Be proud of your creation. Display your portrait at the local art museum, neighborhood library, or family fridge.

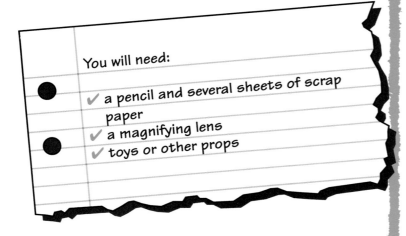

You will need:

✓ a pencil and several sheets of scrap paper
✓ a magnifying lens
✓ toys or other props

What to Do:

Using toys, you can pose your caterpillar as a

Do they bite? Can they swim?

How many times does a caterpillar shed its skin? How many legs do they have? Can they see in the dark?

What do they eat?

Will it go across a bridge? Do they have eyes? Ears? Do they have two heads? What end is the head on?

What is the average length of a caterpillar? Why do they curl up? Is it a defense? Are they asleep when they are curled?

Wondertime

Can they hear? How fast do they walk?

How long does it take for them to turn into a butterfly? How long do they live?

These are some questions that kids in my town asked about caterpillars. Do you have any answers or any questions of your own? If you do, don't let them escape! Simple questions have launched many a wild expedition. Think of the journeys started by questions such as, "What's on the other side of the ocean?" or "How high is this mountain?" For fun, jot down some questions. Who knows where they might lead you!

Are you ready to explore great mysteries? Are you prepared to dive into adventures? If you are, all you need to do is hold onto a caterpillar question. Is there something you'd really like to know about caterpillars? Yes? Well, let that question lead you on a journey. Below are some tips for curious caterpillarologists.

Follow That Question

and creating an experiment of your very own.

—**Scrutinize:** Could you answer your question by looking at caterpillars more closely? For example, if your question was, "Do they have feet?" do you think you might be able to find out by viewing a caterpillar through a magnifying lens?

—**Find an Expert:** Do you know a bug expert? Perhaps a local gardener, agricultural advisor, or high school biology teacher can give you a hand. The answer may be only a phone call away.

—**Research:** Other caterpillarologists in the past may have already asked your question. Maybe the answer to your question is hiding in a book. It may even be in this one. Turn the page and search through the next section. If that doesn't work, look at some other books, or come back to this page and read on.

—**Experiment:** Experiments often arise from questions. *What would happen if. . . ?* Could you answer your questions with an experiment? Check out the chapter called Kid Experiments. You may be enticed into putting on your lab coat

ook at this caterpillar. Can you find eyes, a nose, or a mouth? Can you find legs, wings, or arms? Do they have any parts that you lack?

Posterpillar

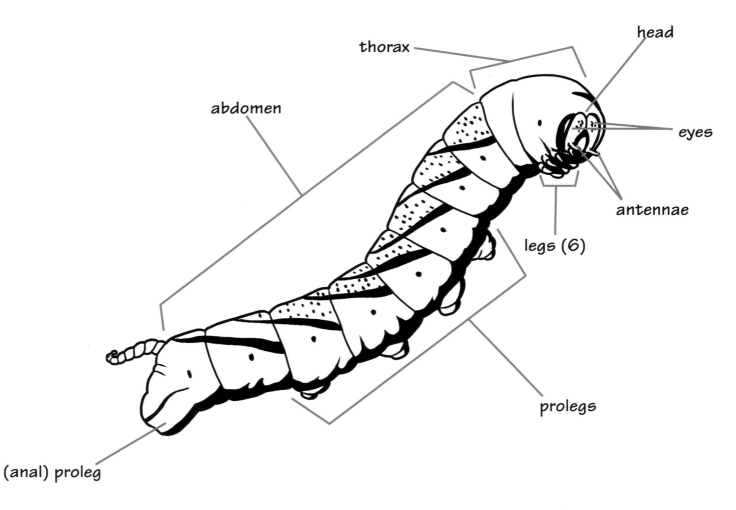

thorax

head

abdomen

eyes

antennae

legs (6)

prolegs

(anal) proleg

Peek inside this caterpillar. Can you discover a stomach or a heart?

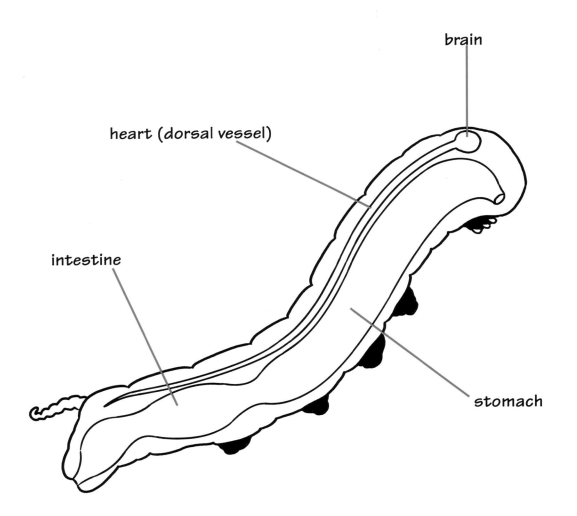

brain

heart (dorsal vessel)

intestine

stomach

What is as skinny as a worm but eats like a pig? What has more legs than a horse but moves as slowly as a snail? What sheds its skin like a snake but grows wings like a bird? Would you believe . . . a caterpillar?

What Is It?

Caterpillars have similarities to all of these animals, but their closest relatives are insects such as bees, beetles, and flies. If you have examined caterpillars closely, you may have noticed that they have six legs, as all insects do. Like that of other insects, the caterpillar's body is divided into three sections: the head, the **thorax,** and the **abdomen.** The head is round and hard. The thorax is divided into three sections, each bearing a pair of jointed legs. The abdomen, composed of ten segments, is the longest part of the caterpillar. If you add up the head, three thorax segments, and ten abdominal segments, how many segments do you get?

Caterpillars are the larvae, or immature stage, of a group of insects called **lepidopterans.** *Lepis* means scale and *pteron* means wing. Moths and butterflies all have scale-covered wings and are thus included in this group.

Caterpillars are not covered with scales, but they do have features that distinguish them from other insect larvae. Unlike fly larvae (called maggots), which are legless, caterpillars have six legs. Unlike beetle larvae (grubs), which have six legs,

caterpillars also have a special set of unjointed, leglike walking stubs called **prolegs.** These are usually found on the third, fourth, fifth, sixth, and last sections of the abdomen. (Inchworms are caterpillars that have prolegs only on the last segment.) The larvae of some wasps also wear prolegs, but theirs lack the special hooks called **crochets** that caterpillars' prolegs have. These clinging hooks help caterpillars to be excellent climbers of stems and leaves.

All insects belong to a larger group of animals called **arthropods.** *Arthro* means "joint" and *pod* means "foot." All arthropods have jointed feet. Millipedes, lobsters, tarantulas, and scorpions are all arthropods and distant cousins of the caterpillar.

Check out your caterpillar and your caterpillar portraits. Does your caterpillar fit the description of a lepidopteran, an insect and an arthropod?

Arthropods are creatures with pairs of jointed legs. The animals below are arthropods.

Crayfishes

Houseflies

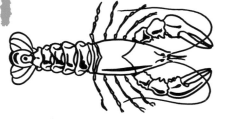

Insects are arthropods with three body parts and three pairs of legs. Most insects have a larval form. The animals below are insects.

Ladybugs

Mosquitoes

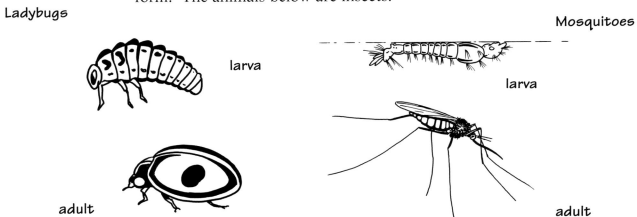

larva

adult

larva

adult

Lepidopterans are insects with scales on their wings. The animals below are lepidopterans.

Moths (Hawkmoth)

Caterpillars (Monarch)

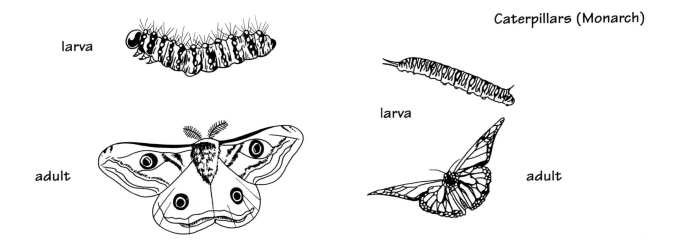

larva

adult

larva

adult

Each language has its own name for caterpillars. In German the word for caterpillar is *Raupe*. In Croat it's *gusjenica*. In Hebrew it's *zahkal*. Is it *Raupe, gusjenica, zahkal,* or caterpillar? To avoid using all these different names, scientists have devised a worldwide system of naming all living things. Whether you live in Germany, Croatia, or Israel, there is only one scientific name for each. This is especially important for caterpillars because many of them are given different common names as adults. For example, the caterpillar known as the tomato hornworm is called the five-spotted hawkmoth later in life.

Latin and Greek, the languages of ancient Rome and Greece, are used in creating scientific names. Most kids already know a few of these names because all dinosaurs are known by the names given to them by scientists. For example, the word *brachiosaurus* comes from the Latin

Zahkal, Gusjenica— Say What?

words *bracchius* (arm) and *saurus* (lizard). The scientific name for the question-mark butterfly, a butterfly with indented wing edges and a question-mark pattern on its underwing, is *Polygonia* (many sided) *interrogationis* (like a question).

Picky Eaters

Though most are leaf-munchers, there are some caterpillars with more exotic diets. Wax-moth caterpillars eat beeswax, and clothes-moth caterpillars eat wool. One type of inchworm in Hawaii actually attacks and eats other insects, and the sloth moth caterpillar eats nothing but sloth scat (*scat* is a scientific word for poop).

Even leaf-eaters are particular about what kind of salad they'll eat. Cabbageworms (the larvae of cabbage butterflies) only devour plants in the cabbage family, while tomato hornworms (the larvae of hawkmoths) stick to tomato plants and their relatives. Other caterpillars, such as the woolly bears (the larvae of tiger moths), will eat plants from several plant groups, but they won't munch on just any old leaf that's placed in front of them. Monarch butterfly caterpillars and their close relatives are among the pickiest of all—they will only eat milkweeds!

Caterpillars are indeed picky eaters, but it doesn't seem to be their fault. Since the days of the dinosaurs, 180 million years ago, plants have been developing defenses against caterpillars and other hungry **herbivores** (ER-buh-vorz), or plant eaters. Over time, many plants have developed chemicals that make their leaves and other parts taste yucky to most insects.

Unfortunately for the plants, some caterpillars have adapted to these new chemicals. For example, to most other animals the sap of the milkweed plant is poison-ous, but not to the monarch caterpillars. Not only are they adjusted to eating this toxic food, but they in turn benefit by becoming poisonous themselves. The milk-weed poisons in their bodies then protect them from being eaten by other animals.

Caterpillars do not usually have to start life searching for food, because they are born right at the dinner table. Moths and butterflies lay their eggs on the types of plants that they ate when they were caterpillars. That way, the new larvae that will hatch out will have the right food available. If a caterpillar runs out of food or falls off a plant, it can find its way to new food through its senses of smell, taste, and touch.

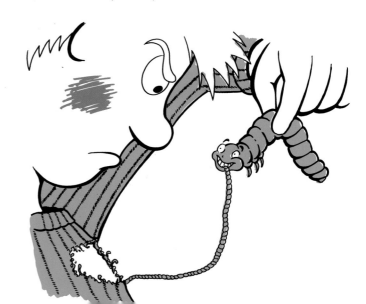

Eating Machines

Some kids have reputations for eating, but those are nothing compared to the appetites of caterpillars. Imagine consuming 86,000 times your birth weight in just 24 days. This is what the caterpillar of the polyphemus moth does. For the average-size human baby, that would be like eating several truckloads of baby food in just a few weeks. With this diet, it's no wonder that caterpillars grow fast. When most caterpillars are born, they are only about 1 millimeter long. By the time they are two months old, they are 2 centimeters long. This may not seem like a major growth spurt, but it's almost a 2000 percent increase in length. This would be like a 1½-foot-long human baby growing as long as a football field!

— 1 mm

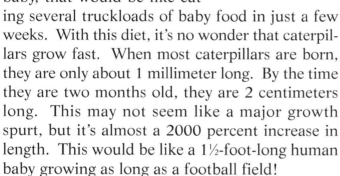

2 cm

(2,000%)

In the process of eating all of this food, caterpillars produce an enormous amount of droppings, called frass. As caterpillars munch, frass falls like hail. Many caterpillars have a special comb on their rears to help them flick away the frass. Without this mechanism, they might literally be buried in their own waste.

Since caterpillars are such major munchers, they can quickly do damage to food crops if their numbers aren't controlled by disease or **predators** (other critters that eat them). The greatest populations of caterpillars appear on large farms where only one crop is grown. On one tea plantation in Java, over 200,000 caterpillars were picked off the tea bushes in just one day. In large cornfields, there can be as many as one million corn earworms per acre!

Famous Transformers

Long before toy transformers were invented, caterpillars were going through much more amazing transformations. While toy transformers require people to make them change from one shape to another, caterpillars go through changes all by themselves. From eggs no bigger than a grain of sand hatch tiny caterpillars. These little wormlike creatures eat and grow until they have become so fat that they are about to burst out of their skins. Instead of expanding to allow growth, the way human skin does, the skin of caterpillars simply splits down the back. Out of the old skin wriggles the caterpillar, leaving it behind like discarded clothes. During the next hour or two, the caterpillar expands itself. Not only is the caterpillar larger after each **molt,** or shedding of skin, but it also looks different. During each of these new growth stages, or **instars,** caterpillars may change color or shape, or even have new features, such as hairs or bumps. All caterpillars go through three to five molts before they are fully grown.

Then the most amazing transformation of all occurs. The caterpillar makes its final molt and changes into a **pupa** (PYOO-pah), which stays attached to a twig or other surface. Moth pupae are brown and often covered in silken cases called **cocoons,** which the larvae have spun around themselves. Butterfly pupae, also called **chrysalises** (KRIH-suh-lis-ez), are multicolored and are attached to twigs or leaves.

Inside the pupal case, a larva changes into an adult. Its hard jaws turn into a long, curled tongue. Its short, stubby legs and its **antennae** grow longer. But the most remarkable change of all is the addition of four large wings.

When the newly formed adult moth or butterfly is ready to emerge, the pupal case cracks, and out crawls a wet, crumpled creature. As blood is pumped into the veins that lace the wings, these flappers expand until they are full size. Once the wings are stiff, the winged adults eat again. At this stage of their lives, they can no longer chew leaves. Instead, using their long, strawlike tongues, they sip nectar, a sweet liquid found in flowers. Nectar is flight fuel, and it provides them with the energy to flutter about. Using their new and improved antennae, they seek out mates. After mating, the females lay eggs, and the cycle is ready to start over. The process of changing forms, from egg to caterpillar to pupa to moth or butterfly, is called **metamorphosis.** Metamorphosis can take from six weeks to a year. Most lepidopterans live less than a year, while some, such as the monarch butterflies, may live through the winter.

Lepidopterans lead two lives with two different body forms. During their lives as caterpillars, they are eating machines. They take in fuel for the growth they need to transform into winged adults that can flap through the air to seek mates and lay eggs.

Presto-Change-o Chart

Caterpillar—	Moth or Butterfly—
Eating Machine	**Mating Machine**
6 fleshy legs	6 thin, hairy legs
6-8 prolegs	4 wings
short antennae	long antennae
chewing mouthparts	coiled, strawlike mouthpart
12 simple eyes	2 compound eyes

4 wings

long antennae

12 simple eyes

short antennae

2 compound eyes

6 long legs

strawlike coiled tongue

6 short legs

6-8 prolegs

A nice juicy caterpillar served on a leaf is the daily snack of many outdoor diners. Robins, chickadees, and wrens eat them by the dozen. For most songbird babies, at least one out of every four meals is caterpillar. Some baby birds, are fed caterpillars for almost every meal.

Fast-Food Favorites

Many **species,** or kinds, of thread-waisted wasps (including the sand wasp in the photo below) paralyze caterpillars by stinging them and injecting poison. The caterpillar, which looks dead but continues to breathe, is then dragged into the wasp's burrow. The wasp next lays eggs on the caterpillar and seals the burrow closed. Later, when the wasp larvae hatch, the caterpillar becomes a living meal. Other wasps, such as braconids, are **parasites** (PAR-uh-syts) on caterpillars. They lay their eggs inside caterpillars. These caterpillars become the **host**—the food source and home—for the wasp larvae when they hatch. These larvae begin chewing up the guts of the helpless host until eventually the caterpillar dies. By this time, the wasp larvae are ready to crawl out of the caterpillar and spin cocoons. When the new adult wasps emerge, off they go in search of more caterpillars to lay eggs in.

In many different parts of the world, caterpillars are even considered a tasty snack by people. In Asia, silk moth caterpillars are a favorite treat.

In Congo, there are a large number of delicious caterpillars to choose from. In California, the large larvae of pandora moths are still collected by Paiutes, a Native American people. These larvae are baked and then dried for future use. Caterpillars are an ideal food. They are low in fat and high in protein. Not all caterpillars are edible, but if you want to see what they taste like, you could try the cabbage looper, a caterpillar found on cabbages, broccoli, and lettuce plants.

Of those fortunate caterpillars that survive to change into pupae, many end up being eaten by small mammals such as shrews and skunks. Those lepidopterans that make it to adulthood may be snagged by bats, birds, or long-tongued toads. It's not easy to survive as one of the natural world's fast-food favorites.

Look at a caterpillar. Does it seem helpless? Do you wonder how it survives hungry hunters in the wild? Examine it again. Does your caterpillar have **camouflage** (KAH-muh-flazh), distasteful qualities, a safe shelter, or chemical weapons?

Clever Defenders

There are green caterpillars, such as army cutworms, that are nearly invisible on the green surfaces of leaves and stems, and brown caterpillars, such as the hemlock spanworm, that blend in with dead leaves and branches. There are even some, such as those of the Japanese swallowtail, that look exactly like bird droppings. This method of disguise is called camouflage, or protective coloring.

Some caterpillars, such as bagworms, cover themselves with bits of leaves, while others, such as grape-leaf folders, use silk to sew leaves into tubes or envelopes where they are hidden from view. Leaf-mining caterpillars seek protection inside leaves and pine needles. Other caterpillars live in plant growths called **galls** that plants make in response to chemicals injected by the mother moth. Inside the ball-shaped gall, the caterpillars are safe from most hunters. Cigar-case bearers and tent caterpillars weave silken shelters for protection.

Though many caterpillars are expertly camouflaged, there are also quite a few that stand out like neon signs. During one instar, when pine caterpillars are bright red, they are easy to spot. One of these caterpillars would be a tasty meal if it wasn't covered with over 600,000 stinging hairs. The caterpillars of the anise swallowtail butterfly are a greenish yellow with black-and-orange markings. When disturbed, they poke out an orange-colored, horn-shaped structure called an **osmeterium** (ahz-meh-TEER-ee-um) and release an obnoxious odor that repels enemies.

Another way to survive is by tasting terrible. Milkweed caterpillars eat milkweeds, which contain poisons that cause most animals to throw up. Thus, though these insects are sometimes tasted, they are seldom eaten. They taste so nasty that birds and other hunters just spit them out.

Have you ever been frightened by a caterpillar? Some large caterpillars are adorned with patterns that make them look like snakes or lizards. At first glance, it's easy for birds and humans to be fooled by this disguise. Check out the colors, patterns, and homes of your local caterpillars. How do you think they survive in the wild?

Silky Lips

Picture yourself climbing on a steep cliff. You are high above the ground, and all of a sudden you let go. Instead of tumbling to your death, you descend slowly by lowering yourself on a fine rope that comes from an opening near your lips. When you reach the ground, you build a tent from this same silky substance. Inside it, you are safe from storms and other dangers.

Unfortunately, we can't make silk, but caterpillars (including the tent caterpillars in the photo below) can. Close to the chompers of caterpillars are small, pointed structures called **spinnerets.** These produce silk, which caterpillars use for making trails, building shelters, making safety lines, and weaving cocoons.

The silk moth caterpillar is the best known of the silk-making caterpillars because it has supplied humans with silken threads for over four thousand years. The Chinese were the first to make silk cloth, and it was such an important business in China that at one time, smuggling silk moth caterpillars to other countries was considered a crime punishable by death.

The caterpillar questions asked by students at the El Portal Elementary school led to some simple but amazing experiments.

Do Caterpillars Prefer One Direction to Another?

One day Nichole watched a checkerspot caterpillar crawl across her desk from the upper right corner to the lower left corner. She returned the caterpillar to the upper right corner, and it cruised back down to the lower left corner again. She repeated this test many times. Sometimes she faced the caterpillar away from the lower left corner when she returned it to the upper right corner, but it would turn around and head in the same direction, which was northwest, each time.

Next, Nichole replaced the first caterpillar with another checkerspot. She started it in the upper right corner and watched where it traveled. After repeating this twice, she tested one more caterpillar. Below are her results, showing the direction the caterpillars traveled during each test.

Kid Experiments

Caterpillar #1	Caterpillar #2	Caterpillar #3
Northwest: 3	Southeast: 2	Northeast: 1
	Southwest: 1	North: 1
		South: 2
		East: 1
		West: 1

Nichole concluded that some caterpillars seem to prefer going in one direction, while others don't. What do you think?

Do Caterpillars Get Dizzy?

Nick wondered what happens to caterpillars when the leaves they live on are blown about in the wind. Do the caterpillars get dizzy? To test this question, Nick used a paper spinner that he made from two paper plates held together with a fastener. For each test, he gave a different caterpillar a whirly ride on his spinner and then watched what it did after the spinner had stopped.

Here are his results:

Caterpillar I: It looked up and all around and walked in circles.
Caterpillar II: It walked forward slowly.
Caterpillar III: It spun off the spinner, so it was disqualified.
Caterpillar IV: It stood still and then looked around.

Nick thought that his experiment showed that caterpillars get dizzy because they acted dizzy. What do you think?

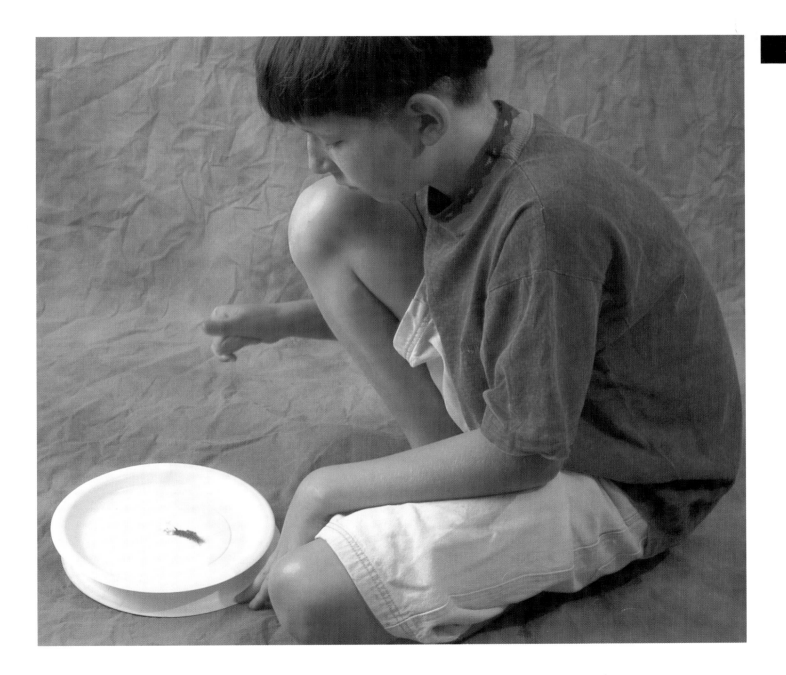

What Causes Caterpillars to Curl Up?

Chris observed that each of the three caterpillars he was watching curled up when he touched it. Did anything else cause them to curl? Chris tried a series of tests with all the caterpillars, and this is what he discovered.

- The caterpillars curled up when he bounced them on a piece of paper.
- When he shook the desk that they were on, they did not curl up.
- When he blew on them, they did not curl up.
- When he placed a finger in front of them, they did not curl up.
- When he placed a pencil inside the curl of a curled-up caterpillar, it held onto the pencil.

Chris thought caterpillars might curl up for warmth or because they are afraid. Do you have any theories about curling caterpillars?

Aaron also wondered how to make caterpillars uncurl. He discovered, after some experimenting, that a curled-up caterpillar would uncurl when tossed gently from hand to hand.

How Do Caterpillars React to Wind?

When Aaron blew on the tail end of a caterpillar, he noticed that it went faster. When he blew on its front end, it waved its head and turned around. He tried it again with three other caterpillars and got the same results with two of them. The other one sped up with a tailwind, but only waved its head in reaction to a head-on breeze. Were the caterpillars reacting just to the breeze or to human bad breath? When Aaron fanned a caterpillar with a piece of paper, it turned away. Why did some of the caterpillars react to the wind? Aaron thought that maybe whenever the wind comes toward caterpillars, it blows leaves at them and they might get hit by the blowing leaves. Maybe they learn to go away from the wind to avoid getting hit on the head. Do you have any ideas about why caterpillars react to wind?

How Fast Does a Caterpillar Go?

Leann and Allison placed caterpillars between two parallel yardsticks and measured how far they went in 45 seconds. They used six different caterpillars and did five tests with each. The results were as follows.

test	Stacy	Jack	Tortice
1	12"	15"	3"
2	5"	15"	3"
3	0"	15"	2.5"
4	0"	17"	2"
5	0"	0"	4"

test	Timmy	Cenady	Earry
1	10"	13"	7"
2	11"	12"	3"
3	12"	11"	4"
4	11"	5"	5"
5	6"	6"	6"

As you can see, the fastest one only went 17 inches in 45 seconds. At this rate, it would take Jack almost two days to travel one mile! Do you think other kinds of caterpillars might walk faster or slower? Why?

What Can a Caterpillar Climb?

Josh found out that a caterpillar could climb a branch. Rhyen discovered that a caterpillar could climb up his arm, and Claire watched one travel uphill on her dress. Ali placed one in a plastic cup and watched as it tried to clamber up, but alas, after a few minutes it had made no progress. What else do you think a caterpillar can climb? Why do you think caterpillars are good climbers?

Hansel and Gretel Caterpillars

Over one hundred years ago, scientist Henri Fabre investigated the unusual behavior of pine processionary caterpillars, which he kept in a special laboratory outside his home in the south of France. In the evenings, these fuzzy red caterpillars march like parades of British redcoats from their silk-covered nests to the pine trees where they feed. With a leader in front, each trails along in single file, following the silken thread laid down by the caterpillar in ahead of it.

Fabre carefully watched these marching larvae for many evenings. He observed the caterpillars as they left the nest each evening and soon discovered that any caterpillar that ended up in front of the others would become the leader. He also observed that though these caterpillars occasionally wander from their paths, they usually follow the silk trails like commuters on a highway. The more Fabre watched, the more he wondered. What if the caterpillars lost their leader? What if they lost their path the way Hansel and Gretel lost their trail of bread crumbs? To find out, he conducted several experiments.

In one test, Fabre removed the leader of one line and discovered that the second in line immediately took its place as the new leader. It didn't pause to wonder where its leader went. It just kept going as if there hadn't been a change. In another experiment, Fabre removed a caterpillar from the middle of one marching line and carefully cut and removed a section of the silken path with scissors. The first half of the caterpillar parade moved on, but the second half veered off with a new leader on a new path of its own. Fabre repeated this experiment several times. In some tests the two groups met and joined together, and in others they stayed separate. Why do you think the caterpillars behaved differently?

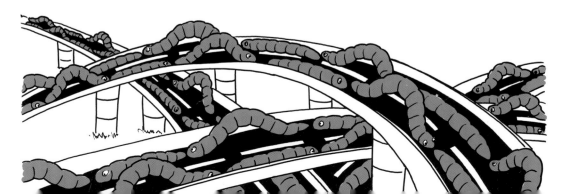

In science-fiction movies, alien creatures sometimes take over the bodies of earthlings. In real life, there are wasps that take over the bodies of caterpillars. The wormlike larvae of these parasitic wasps get both room and board (food) as they eat the guts of the caterpillars. Getting eaten from the inside out is not very healthy for caterpillars, and they eventually die. By this time, however, the wasp larvae have usually crawled out and made cocoons. Inside the cocoon, each wasp larva transforms into a pupa, which then becomes a winged adult wasp.

Body Snatchers and Body Guards

Jacques Brodeur and Louise Vet, two scientists from the Netherlands who study parasitic wasps, noticed something very strange. Some caterpillars stayed alive even after the wasp parasites crawled out of their bodies to make cocoons. In addition, these caterpillars made webs over the wasp cocoons lying next to them. When Jacques and Louise touched the almost-dead caterpillars, they thrashed about madly as if they were fighting off an enemy. Why were these caterpillars acting so strange? Why was their behavior so different from that of other caterpillars parasitized by wasps? Did the wasp larvae have anything to do with the caterpillars' odd behavior?

To find some answers, Jacques and Louise set up a series of tests. They used cabbage butterfly caterpillars and two species of *Cotesia* wasps. All the caterpillars were placed on brussels sprout plants, where they munched leaves. The caterpillars were separated into two groups. One group was allowed to be parasitized by *Cotesia rubecula*. The other was attacked by a different species, *Cotesia glomerata*.

After several weeks, Jacques and Louise noticed that the larvae of *Cotesia rubecula* were crawling out of the caterpillars. The wasp larvae then made cocoons on the ground. The caterpillars crawled away and soon died.

A few weeks after that, the larvae of *Cotesia glomerata* began popping out of caterpillars that were almost ready to make cocoons. The wasp larvae made their own cocoons on the ground right next to the caterpillars, and instead of wandering away, these caterpillars curled around the wasp cocoons and wove silk coverings over them. When Jacques and Louise tickled these caterpillars with a brush, they thrashed about, bit at the brush, and spat out drops of red fluid. Were they protecting the wasp cocoons like a dog defending its master's home? Wasp pupae are also often attacked by other parasitic wasps. Were these pupae being protected by the thrashing caterpillars?

Jacques and Louise thought so. When they discovered that these caterpillars died only after the wasp pupae had safely turned into adults, they were even more certain.

Like police surgeons, Jacques and Louise examined the insides of the dead caterpillars. Those killed by *Cotesia rubecula* were missing most of their vital parts, while those killed by *Cotesia glomerata* had many parts remaining. Enough damage had been done to prevent these caterpillars from making full cocoons, but the caterpillars still had enough pep to make some silk and to chase away predators. It appeared to Louise and Jacques that just as aliens that invade human bodies in sci-fi movies, *Cotesia glomerata* larvae had changed the behavior of the caterpillars they had

invaded. The wasps had turned the caterpillars into guards that would protect them while they were in their cocoons. They had made the caterpillars protect their own killers!

Many farmers use toxic chemicals called pesticides to kill caterpillars that are munching crops. Pesticides can also harm the people who eat the crops or work in the fields. Natural enemies, such as wasps, can also be used to kill caterpillars without poisoning people. Scientists such as Louise and Jacques are learning to make it easier for parasitic wasps to dine on caterpillars. Now they know that some wasps even get help from the caterpillars that they kill.

Henri Fabre was fascinated by the faithful following of the caterpillars he studied, and he tried to set up an experiment to see what would happen if the caterpillars ended up on a circular track. Would they keep going forever, around and around, or would they soon break away from the never-ending path? Using tweezers, he tried to pick up some of the silken trails and arrange them in a circle, but they were too fragile, and they fell apart. Finally one day, Fabre discovered a parade of caterpillars winding around the top of a vase in which a palm was growing. Just before the leader had made the full circuit around the top, Henri quickly brushed away the trail that connected the silken circle to the bottom of the pot. This was the trail they had taken up to the top of the pot, and Fabre thought they would go back down it once they made a full circuit around the pot. With this escape trail gone, the lead caterpillar now ended up at the beginning of the circle, close behind the last caterpillar in the line. Every caterpillar was now following another like horses on a merry-go-round. The more they marched, the more silk

Circle Tour

they dribbled onto the trail, and the thicker it grew.

How long would they continue following each other in this endless circle? Fabre thought that they would veer off the path in an hour or two when they became hungry or tired, but he discovered otherwise. That first day, they marched on and on like weary hikers. To tempt them off their path, Fabre placed a branch of pine needles only a hand's length away. After keeping an eye on them for ten hours, he went off to bed. In the morning, instead of finding them feeding on the pine needles, he discovered that they were still on their path. In fact, they remained on their circle trail for another six days. A few times some of them wandered a little way off the trail, but never far enough to find food. Each time, the trailblazers returned and, wearier than ever, continued their hopeless march. Finally, a few wandered farther off the trail and led the exhausted group back to the nest.

Though they may seem stupid, pine processionary caterpillars have survived for millions of years. Do you think Fabre's experiment was a fair test of their ability to deal with problems?

Though scientists have solved some caterpillar puzzles, there are many more mysteries to explore. Remember those questions you jotted down? Have all of them been answered? Even common creatures such as caterpillars that have been living in our backyards forever have secrets waiting to be revealed by curious, ingenious caterpillarologists.

Questions that are easily explored may offer fast rewards, but true mysteries are exciting to uncover, like hidden treasure. Consider your mysterious questions once more and imagine the wild adventures they could lead to.

Below are some challenging questions that kids from my town may still be investigating at this very moment.

Can a caterpillar get sick from eating too much food?

Will a caterpillar go through a tunnel?

Will a caterpillar go away from noise?

Can they see in the dark?

Are caterpillars smart?

What leftover questions do you have?

Glossary

abdomen: the rear section of an insect's body

antennae: sense organs found in pairs on the heads of some animals, including insects

arthropods: a large group of animals that includes insects, spiders, and some shellfish

camouflage: a way of disguising something by making it blend it with its surroundings

chrysalis: another name for butterfly pupae

cocoons: silken cases that some moth larvae spin around themselves, inside of which they turn into pupae

crochets: hooklike structures found on the prolegs of caterpillars

frass: the solid waste of caterpillars and other insects

galls: swollen growths in plants

herbivores: animals that live on a diet of plants

host: an animal whose body provides food and a home to another animal

instars: the period between the molts of a larvae

larvae: insects in an early growth stage

lepidopterans: a group of scale-winged insects that includes moths and butterflies

metamorphosis: a change from one form to another

molt: the shedding of skin, fur, or feathers

osmeterium: a structure on the bodies of some caterpillars through which they release a bad-smelling substance

parasite: an animal that harms another animal, called a host, by depending upon it for food

predators: animals that hunt, kill, and eat other animals

prolegs: leglike stubs found on the abdomens of some insect larvae

pupae: insects in a growth stage just before adulthood

species: a group of animals with common traits, especially the means of creating young

spinnerets: organs on the bodies of some animals, including caterpillars, that produce silk

thorax: the middle section of an insect's body

Index

About the Author

For over twenty years, Michael Elsohn Ross has taught visitors to Yosemite National Park about the park's wildlife and geology. Mr. Ross, his wife, Lisa (a nurse who served nine seasons as a ranger-naturalist), and their son, Nick, have led other families on wilderness expeditions from the time Nick learned to crawl. Mr. Ross studied conservation of natural resources at the University of California/Berkeley, with a minor in entomology (the study of insects). His other books for children include the Naturalist's Apprentice series, also published by Carolrhoda.

Mr. Ross makes his home on a bluff above the wild and scenic Merced River, at the entrance to Yosemite. His backyard garden is a haven for rolypolies, crickets, snails, worms, caterpillars, ladybugs, and a myriad of other intriguing critters.